IMAGES
of Wales

LLANELLI
RUGBY CLUB

The long record of success against overseas touring teams began with the defeat of the Maoris, 1888/9, by a dropped goal to nil. Harry Bowen found the posts from the halfway line.

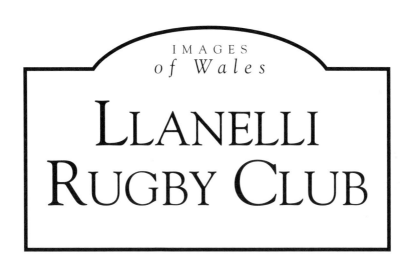

IMAGES
of Wales

LLANELLI
RUGBY CLUB

Compiled by
Bob Harragan

TEMPUS

Tempus Publishing Limited
The Mill, Brimscombe Port,
Stroud, Gloucestershire, GL5 2QG

ISBN 0 7524 1134 9

Typesetting and origination by
Tempus Publishing Limited
Printed in Great Britain by
Midway Clark Printing, Wiltshire

Llanelly No. 8, Harry Truman, is in the thick of the action in this wartime international between Wales and England which was played at Gloucester in 1943.

Contents

Acknowledgements

This collection of photographs would not have been possible were it not for the availability of the superb archives at Llanelli Public Library. Many thanks to Carmarthenshire County Council and their Cultural Services Manager David Griffiths, Llanelli Area Librarian Richard Davies, Reference Librarian Phillip Connell, and library staff Jean Phillips and Yvonne Jones. I have also had much help from Steve Williams, son of Wales and British Lions forward R.H. Williams, who has spent many years collecting things connected with his father's career. Thanks too, to Harry Davies and to Gareth Hughes, whose two detailed histories *One Hundred Years of Scarlet* and *The Scarlets* have been of invaluable help.

Introduction

Llanelli has always been synonymous with running, attacking rugby and has also been proudly parochial. A native of the town has little doubt that the way things are done here is far better than the way they are done elsewhere and over the years, the rugby players have performed in a way that backs up this belief.

Llanelli – the 'y' being replaced by the more pure Welsh 'i' in the 1960s – was a metalworking town, a hum of activity caused by the industrial revolution. The coal from the Gwendraeth Valley was brought down to the town where it helped to make copper and steel, but most of all tin. Llanelly was called 'Tinopolis' at the height of its fame.

The *nouveau riche* mine and works' owners came out of the burgeoning public school system and with them they brought the game of rugby; the early players were the 'crachach' – the toffs of the town. It was a while before they began to play in a scarlet jersey; one early strip contained a primrose stripe and many players preferred to play in their shirtsleeves.

Most of the early fixtures were against teams we would not recognize today, but early matches were played against Llanelly's near neighbour Swansea. The love/hate relationship between Swansea, 'The Jacks', and Llanelli, they called us 'Turks', continues to this day.

The early team had much success and twice won the Welsh Rugby Union's first Challenge Cup. Even then, there were complaints that Welsh selectors much preferred players from more socially acceptable places like Cardiff and Newport to play in international teams. It was a rough and ready game and the early teams were often accused of rough play which today we would call commitment. John Lewis, 'Johnny Bach', the first great favourite of the crowd and spiritual ancestor of Phil Bennett, recalled playing a Swansea team whose full-back played on crutches. He would fling them away before crouching for a tackle. Full-back, Ned Roberts, once borrowed a spectator's overcoat during a snow-driven January match.

The scarlet jersey was introduced in the 1890s and the team soon earned the nickname of 'The Scarlet Runners'. The legend of Llanelli rugby was born in December 1888, when the first touring Maori side was beaten, 3 – 0. The points were scored by full-back, D. Harry Bowen, with a drop goal from the halfway line. Bowen, a schoolteacher, spent time in Yorkshire and may well have been an influence on the Welsh player's attraction to the Northern clubs. From this split with the Northern Union came the creation of Rugby League.

By the 1890s, this team of patricians was getting out of touch. Many of the best rugby players were ordinary workmen from the tinplate mills, but they were not welcome in the snobbish atmosphere of Stradey. Standards began to fall. The problem was finally solved when the more enlightened officials negotiated an amalgamation with Seaside Stars. Within a year, four of the Stars, officially a junior club, had been picked for Wales.

One of the leading Seaside players was Ben Davies, whose son Harry wrote about the Scarlets' deeds for the *Evening Post* in Swansea throughout the 1950s, '60s, '70s and early '80s. He tells one light-hearted tale of the gulf between the gentleman backs and the working class forwards: 'Hopkin Thomas, my headmaster, took the 2nd XV to Swansea soon after they had suffered a bad defeat when 'The Jacks' came to Stradey. He called the team together. "The match at Stradey was a debacle," he told them. "We cannot have it happen again." As he took to the field he called them together again. "We must not have another debacle," he reminded them. One of the forwards, who had little education, went over to the pack leader and said: "Which one is this Dai Backle then?" The pack leader pointed to a giant, red-headed Swansea forward. "That's him there." The forward took the red-head out of the game and that was one of the main reasons Llanelly won.'

The Llanelly legend was reinforced in 1908 when the Australians were beaten, 8 – 3. After the First World War came a new legend, Albert Jenkins, whose twinkling feet have been the benchmark for Llanelly backs ever since. In 1926, the Maoris were beaten again. Through the years of depression, thousands would wend their way to Stradey, clutching the sixpence that would get them on to the 'tanner' bank. New heroes arose such as Ernie Finch and Bill Clement, but few were more loved than Elvet Jones, the flying winger whose talents were recognized by the British Lions before the Welsh selectors.

In the 1950s, there was R.H. Williams, the giant Wales and Lions forward. His son, Steve, has spent years researching his father's career and it is thanks to his work that so much of that era can be shown here. This was also a time when Handel Rogers, the genial postmaster from Swansea Road, was a giant in the administration of the club. He pioneered Llanelly's trips overseas which started with a bang with the tour to Moscow for the World Student Games in the 1950s.

Enthusiasm for rugby has not been at a peak in Llanelli for the club's entire 120 year history however. At times it was even eclipsed by the town's soccer club. Yet in the 1970s, it was almost a religion. The history-making victory over New Zealand's All Blacks, something achieved by no other club side, was followed by a decade of Cup Finals and stunning rugby. When I was a young journalist, sixteen names were more important than anyone else. They began with Carwyn James, and went on: Barry Llewellyn, Roy 'Shanto' Thomas, Tony Crocker, Delme Thomas, Derek Quinnell, Tom David, Hefin Jenkins, Gareth Jenkins, Ray 'Chico' Hopkins, Phil Bennett, Andy Hill, Ray Gravell, Roy Bergiers, J.J. Williams, and Roger Davies. They were giants, but they walked the streets of the town. You would see them in Woolworths, or at the bank and they would stop to gossip with contemporaries who worked in the factories. It was part of being a Llanelli rugby player that the town possessed you.

Twenty years on, we can see that the great days of the 1970s were a final fling of a great industrial power house. Nowadays the works are gone. Our best players, now professional, have had to move away. No longer are there thousands working within yards of the gates of Stradey Park. As they struggle to come to terms with the demands of professional rugby, the new administrators at Stradey have the unenviable task of balancing the expectations of the man in the street with the enormous running costs of a seven day a week business. We must wish them all well.

One

9 – 3

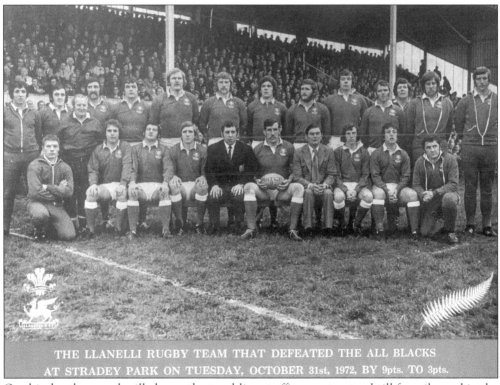

THE LLANELLI RUGBY TEAM THAT DEFEATED THE ALL BLACKS AT STRADEY PARK ON TUESDAY, OCTOBER 31st, 1972, BY 9pts. TO 3pts.

On this day the crowd spilled over the touchline, traffic was at a standstill for miles and in the post match celebrations the pubs were drunk dry – twice!

It was much easier to see when you were a photographer with permission to run the touchline. This view of a lineout, taken from the crowd, gives a better idea of how many people were packed into the ground.

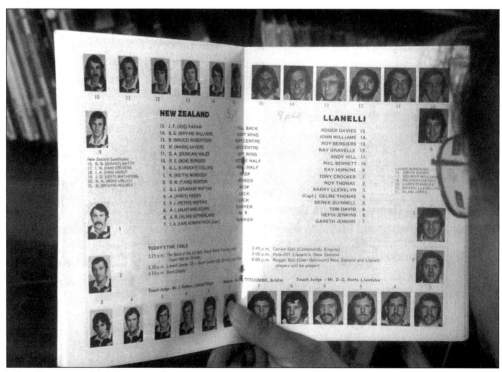

NEW ZEALAND

15. J. F. (JOE) KARAM	FULL BACK	
14. B. G. (BRYAN) WILLIAMS	RIGHT WING	
13. B. (BRUCE) ROBERTSON	RIGHT CENTRE	
12. M. (MARK) SAYERS	LEFT CENTRE	
11. D. A. (DUNCAN) HALES	LEFT WING	
10. R. E. (BOB) BURGESS	OUTSIDE HALF	
9. G. L. (LINDSAY) COLLING	INSIDE HALF	
1. K. (KEITH) MURDOCH	PROP	
2. R. W. (TANE) NORTON	HOOKER	
3. G. J. (GRAHAM) WHITING	PROP	
4. A. (ANDY) HADEN	LOCK	
5. P. J. (PETER) WHITING	LOCK	
6. A. J. (ALISTAIR) SCOWN	FLANKER	
8. A. R. (ALAN) SUTHERLAND	No. 8	
7. I. A. (IAN) KIRKPATRICK (Capt.)	FLANKER	

New Zealand Substitutes:
16. G. B. (GRANT) BATTY
17. L. N. (IAN) STEVENS
18. I. A. (IAN) HURST
19. J. D. (JEFF) MATHESON
20. R. A. (RON) URLICH
21. B. (BEVAN) HOLMES

LLANELLI

ROGER DAVIES	15.	
JOHN WILLIAMS	14.	
ROY BERGIERS	13.	
RAY GRAVELLE	12.	
ANDY HILL	11.	
PHIL BENNETT	10.	
RAY HOPKINS	9.	
TONY CROCKER	1.	
ROY THOMAS	2.	
BARRY LLEWELYN	3.	
(Capt.) DELME THOMAS	4.	
DEREK QUINNELL	5.	
TOM DAVID	6.	
HEFIN JENKINS	8.	
GARETH JENKINS	7.	

Llanelli Substitutes:
16. GWYN ASHBY
17. SELWYN WILLIAMS
18. MEURSON DAVIES
19. CHRIS CHARLES
20. BRYAN LLEWELYN
21. ALAN JAMES

TODAY'S TIME TABLE

1.15 p.m. The Band of the 1st Bn. Royal Welch Fusiliers Town Hall for Stride.
1.30 p.m. Llanelli (under 15) v. Neath (under 15) 30 mins. each way
2.15 p.m. Band Display

2.45 p.m. Canan Gan (Community Singing)
3.00 p.m. Kick-Off Llanelli v. New Zealand
8.00 p.m. Rugger Ball (Glen Ballroom) New Zealand and Llanelli players will be present

Touch Judge : Mr. J. Palfour, Llanelli Kaye   Referee : Mr. TITCOMBE, Bristol   Touch Judge : Mr. D. G. Watts, Llandybie

Llanelli went wild following the 1972 victory over New Zealand's All Blacks. The programme records the names of the fifteen most famous men in the history of the town – not to forget the extraordinary coach, Carwyn James.

In those days gods walked the earth. Phil Bennett epitomized the Llanelli rugby star who never let fame go to his head. He still lives on the outskirts of his home village of Felinfoel, and is ready to pass the time of day with anyone.

'If you win today your names will be remembered in this town 100 years from today,' coach Carwyn James told his team before their match with the All Blacks in 1972. Few of these players have lived on to have such an effect on rugby as the giant Derek Quinnell, whose two sons followed him into the Welsh team.

The Scarlets' victory sent shock waves around the world. A club team beating New Zealand was virtually unprecedented.

6th ANNIVERSARY OF LLANELLI'S
DEFEAT OF NEW ZEALAND

LLANELLI 9pts, NEW ZEALAND 3
Tuesday, October 30th, 1972
(3 PAGES)

Some scenes from the match as recorded by the local press. 'The crowd were so close it seemed like they were on the pitch with us,' said Andy Hill. 'How could we lose? They were just fifteen men and we were 25,000 strong.'

Three of the heroes of the day: Ray Gravell (left), Andy Hill (centre), who kicked the penalty which put the final nail in the All Blacks' coffin and Phil Bennett, (bottom right).

14

J.J Williams, a junior sprint champion, had joined the club, transferring from Bridgend in 1972. A few weeks after the All Blacks match he made his debut as a Wales right-winger and was a fixture with Llanelli and the national side throughout the 1970s.

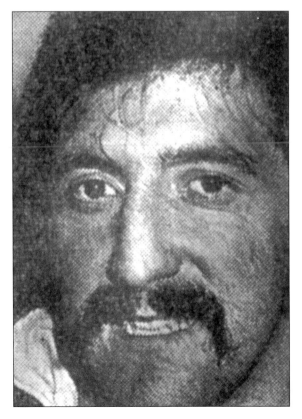

Tommy David, a tireless flank-forward from Pontypridd.

It was a strange unearthly day with an oddly yellow sky. A day when strange things seemed likely to happen.

Flanker Gareth Jenkins, standing fourth from the right, had been spotted as an exceptional talent while still a youngster at Stebonheath school.

'We all had doctor's papers' – Max Boyce.

Skipper Delme Thomas, with the cup and to his left Roy Bergiers, the centre who scored the
only try of the match.

More relaxing times. The victory made celebrities out of the fifteen players. Derek Quinnell (on the back row, sixth from the left), Phil Bennett (on the front row, fourth from the left), Ray Gravell (on the back row, third from the right), and the comedian Stan Stennett (on the back row third from the left) are seen here with a host of others at a charity cricket match at Stradey.

234. – VISIT OF NEW ZEALAND RUGBY FOOTBALL TOURING TEAM

Before commencing the proceedings on the Agenda, His Worship The Mayor (Alderman Gwilym Gibby) referred to the historic victory of the Llanelli Rugby Team over the New Zealand Tourists by 9 points to 3 points at Stradey Park, Llanelli, on the 31st October 1972.   His Worship expressed the pride and pleasure of the people of Llanelli on this unique achievement during the Club's Centenary Year.

All members warmly supported the comments of The Mayor, and it was Resolved – That the congratulations of the Town Council be conveyed to the Llanelli Rugby Football Club.

It was a great day for Llanelli's pride, as both Llanelli Borough Council and Llanelli Rural District Council realized.

Delme Thomas told his team, 'Those people who queued to get in since 8.30 this morning – it's their club as well,' in an emotional speech which had many of them running on to the field in tears. Emotions were also high as he celebrated a Welsh cup victory.

Two

The Scarlet Runners

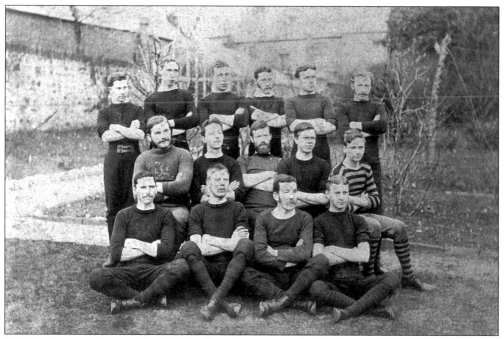

The first known photograph of a Llanelly rugby team, probably taken in 1880. On the back row, from left to right: Henry Margrave, R. Evans, Frank Powell, Fred Margrave, W.B. Roderick, and George Watkeys. Seated: D. John, T. Pyle, Alfred Cattell (later the chairman of Sheffield United football club), H. Mitchell, and S. Roderick. On the ground: Dan Thomas, W. Mitchell, H.L. Sails, and Tom Jones.

Date	Opponents	Ground	Result	Score for Llanelly			Against		
				G.	T				
85'									
ht 5	Eighteen of the District	Llanelly	Won	1	4	10	1		
				18	36				
12	Next Eighteen	Llanelly	Won		4	4	-		
					36				
19	Batley	Llanelly	Lost		2	3	1	1	c
26	Neath	Neath	Won	1	-	1			
t 3	Runcorn	Llanelly	Lost	2	2	7	1	-	
				36	18	7			
10	Swansea	Swansea	Draw	1	-	3	1	-	
24	Newport.	Llanelly	Won	2	-	4	-	1	-
31	Lampeter	Lampeter	Lost		1	2	1	1	2
v 7	Swansea	Llanelly	Won	1	3	8	-	-	1

The early results were recorded in this ledger, now in the Llanelli Library collection, which is thought to have been compiled by D. Harry Bowen.

Points Rangs Opp	Tries got by	Tries kicked by	Goals	Drop Goals by	Rema
64 9	D. H. Bowen	E. J. Powell	1		Fin
	D. Griffiths	Dº	-		
	S. R. Williams	Dº	-		
	Joseph John	Dº	-		
	Joseph John	W B Roderick	-		
40 "	S. R. Williams	E. J. Powell	-		Ka
	D. H. Bowen	Dº	-		
	Geo Watkeys	Dº	-		
	S. R. Williams	Dº	-		
21 30	P. Mitchell	E. J. Powell	-		Fin
√	J. Jones.	Dº	-		His
19 1	J. Watkeys	W. B. Roderick	1		His
61 12	S. R. Williams	W B Roderick	-		
	Fred. L. Margan	W B Roderick	-		
	Wm Thomas	D H Bowen	1		
	Evan Roberts	D H Bowen	1		
21 18	Wm Thomas	D H Bowen	1		Fin
34 9	E. Roberts	D H Bowen	1		
			1	D H Bowen	
11 29	Jos John	D H Bowen	-		Wet
53 1	W. Thomas	D H Bowen	-		His
	Walter Pitt	D H Bowen	1		
		D H B			

23

William Yalden Nevill (centre, left), whose family owned copper smelting and shipbuilding works in Llanelly, was elected to the position of secretary of the new Llanelly Rugby Club when it was formed in 1875. He was also one of the more prominent players. When rugby in the town faded, Nevill is credited with keeping it alive at Felinfoel, with matches played on the park of his home at Westfa House. Llewelyn John, seen sitting on his right in this Felinfoel cricket team, was a Scarlets' full-back.

Another team from the 1880s, photographed on the same spot. The characters are, on the back row, from left to right: H.L. Sails, W. Mitchell, R. Evans, D.W. Evans, Alfred Cattell, and George Watkeys. On the middle row: Thomas Pyle, A. John, T. Jones, F.N. Powell, and H. Mitchell. On the front row: H. Margrave, F.L. Margrave, W.B. Roderick, and S. Roderick.

24

J.G.Lewis – known to the crowd as 'Johnny Bach' – was the first of many charismatic fly-halfs to make a mark at Stradey. He played for Wales against Ireland at Birkenhead Park in 1887, and he worked in one of the many Llanelly tinworks.

His brother, G.P., who played at full-back, went on to become a headmaster in Burry Port.

Llanelly won the South Wales Challenge Cup in 1884, beating Newport in the final. The team was: G.P. Lewis, D. Harry Bowen, John Howell, Frank Powell, W.B. Roderick, F.L. Margrave, J.G. Lewis, Billy Mitchell, Ned Roberts, J. Carruthers, W. Griffiths, T. Jones, Jos Jones, A. Smith, and H. Mitchell.

EASTER HOLIDAYS.

Grand Football Matches!

At the STRADEY GROUNDS, Llanelly.

SATURDAY, April 4th, 1885,
GERMAN GYMNASIUM (LONDON) v. LLANELLY.
GOWER ROAD v. LLANELLY 2ND XV.

EASTER MONDAY, April 6th, 1885,
DEWSBURY (YORKSHIRE) v. LLANELLY.
NEATH 2ND XV. v. LLANELLY 2ND XV.

Kick off (each day) at 3.30 p.m.
Admission—SIXPENCE.
No change given at the gate. No dogs allowed on the ground.

Cheap Tickets will be issued by the Great Western Railway to Llanelly, to witness the above Matches, from Swansea, Carmarthen, Llandilo, and all intermediate Stations.

Tickets for the ground may now be obtained of Mr. John Jones, hairdresser, Station Road, Llanelly.

The Margrave brothers were part of Llanelly's life for many years; their years of sporting prowess were followed by an era when they were among the leading businessmen in the town.

Fred Margrave was the first captain of Llanelly and was also picked to play for Wales.

Surprisingly, no pictorial records exist of the thousands of fans who, often supported by a brass band, would parade the team all the way through town to the Thomas Arms Hotel, where the victors would appear on the balcony. This is in fact a crowd of strikers at the station, but it gives an idea of the likely scene.

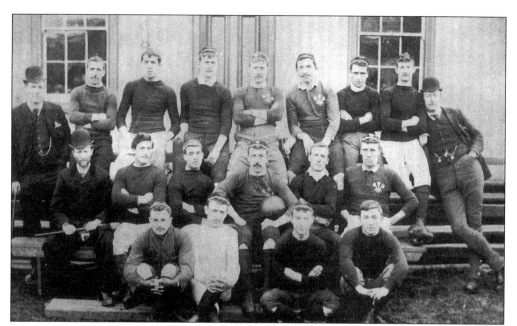

'Johnny Bach' was captain of this team, 1887/8, which included three other Welsh caps.

Industrialist H.R. Thomas claimed to be the man who had introduced rugby football to Llanelly as early as 1872. He also claimed to have paid for the purpose built 'Oval' in People's Park in which early knockabout games were played.

Llanelly railway station was often crowded with fans welcoming a visiting team or welcoming home a victorious Scarlets side.

F.N. Powell, solicitor and all-round sportsman, was a three-quarter who played in many early matches including the Cup Final at the Gnoll, 1880/1. He can be seen on the back row, fourth from the left. Twice in the 1880s, he scored tries in Cup Finals, but ended up on the losing side.

The team's first matches were played on a purpose built 'Oval' in People's Park. The Town Hall was built over the playing area at the turn of the century.

Visiting teams would travel up to the town by horse tram.

THE WINNING OF THE CUP

A BACKER'S EXPERIENCE

To be sung to the tune that Newport died of.

Time, February 27, 7 pm., outside the Newport G.P.O.

Have you heard who's won the Cup for Season 85 and '6
For I'm a Newport backer, and I'm in a dreadful fix;
I have backed Newport heavily, and 'twill be a blooming go
If Newport lose: I'll have to pay the money, don't you kno'!
Though I *know* they've won the battle, quite confident I am;
But why in the name of goodness don't they send a telegram?
I've waited just two hours for the joyful news to come,
So on the strength of winning, I'll just have a glass of rum.

The telegram not yet arrived! Why I begin to fear
That when our team arrive by train the Cup may not be here;
But they will surely win the match, for see, they've all prepared
To give them a reception, and to have captain chaired;
They'll light the place with torches and march right through the town,
All singing 'Newport's won the match! Llanelly has gone down!'
Ah! Now the train is coming in, and I will quickly see
How many goals and tries we scored, how man a minor p.

There's my friend Tom, he's been to see the Final Match to-day,
I'll buckle up 'longside of him and hear what he's to say.
'Oh! I say, Tom, you lucky dog! you've seen the Final Tie!
I bet you're happy now, old man; but, chappie, by-the-bye,
What was the score—the real score? They piled it on, I bet!'
'They did!' said Tom, and in a way I never shall forget;
'For once they fairly started, they piled it on, I swear,
In a way I calculated that raised each backer's hair!'

'I thought as much, old boy, I know Llanelly would go down,
When Monk came down from Cambridge, and Jordan came from town.
But entered they a protest? No, Hurrah for Newport then
For now we've got the Challenge Cup for '86 and 7.
We now are champions of South Wales! and I my bets have won.
The winners I've been fly to back; the fun has just begun,
I breathe once more, so now give me a few points of the play
In answer to my questions in a quiet sort of way.

'How many goals did Arthur drop upon the Swansea ground?
How many tries did Jordan get, how many times ran round?
How many did Bob Gould kick from tries that Jordan got?
How many times did Bailey dodge right through the blooming lot?
How many men that Harding smashed, how many hacks he gave?
How many times the ball came back, and how did dear Webb save?
How many times our forwards rushed, and how behaved Row-ly?
And how many men it took to lift our captain shoulder high?

'How did the crowd behave? and did the people roar
When Arthur dropp'd the ball, and 'twixt the sticks'twas seen the soar?
How did they look when time was called, and how did they feel, old man?
And were they quite as confident as when the game began?
How many bets did you get on, and *how much* did you win?
How many people were on the field, and how many taken in?
How many tinmen came be train, and how many folk by tram?
And how in the name of Moses didn't they send the telegram?

'I see that I perplex you, so in order to be brief,
I'll fish up now some of the points the Scarlets brought to grief:
How many goals did Arthur drop? or dropp'd he more than one?
Brief by plain, the answer came, in mournful accents' None.'
'The match was won by tries; pray, how many tries in all?'
Brief, but plain, the answer came, 'Proportionately small.'
'Then if we won by minor points, we must have got a lot!'
'The minor points that Newport scored are clearly shown by 0.'

'No goals, no tries, no minor points—why, what is this you say?
You'll tell me next the Newport men have lost the match to-day!
I know you're only jesting, for see, here's all prepared
To give them a reception, an the have the captain chair'd;
But if they've lost the match to-day—the thought makes my blood freeze—
We'll dip them in the muddy Usk, and burn their effigies;
I thought Llanelly team a frost, by though there's been a thaw,
I still shall be contented if the match has been a draw.

Then spoke the suffering Thomas: 'Brother backer, list to me,—
I've seen a *game* of football played, but a *match* I didn't see;
I've seen Monk try to drop a goal from middle of the ground,
I have seen Bailey try to dodge, and Jordan try to round,
But I've seen all these failing, yes, failing ev'ry one;
They were germs of good intentions, but were squashed where they'd begun;
I've seen dear Webb, the sprinter, mess the ball, without a doubt;
And if you've any money down, take my advice–shell out.

'I've seen our forwards *try* to rush, that's the only *try* they scored;
I've seen the ball soar 'twixt the posts, and how the people roared;
A furthermore, my backer dear, I've seen who sent that ball,
'Twas a player they called Harry, who was smiley, cool, and tall;
He spoke in soothing whispers, but he made his language plain
And convincing to Newportians, when he sent it through again;
I've seen that Bowen's brother of his sole chance make the most,
And sending from quite mid-distance, the ball against the post.

'I've seen a *man* called Sammy, and a man called Gitto too;
I've seen the Prince of Wales perform at half-back, so have you;
I've seen that Rowly Hill disallow a splendid try,
Got by a man called John—Johnny Howells, by the by;
I've seen a boy of 9 stone stop a man of fully 11;
I need not tell you that, that boy was rather more than 7;
I've seen the tinplate partisans—strange things I've seen this day!
The things I am recounting in a quiet sort of way.

'I see you wish to question, and I know what you would ask;
"Where were the Newport forwards, and didn't they do their task?
Did they not push? did they not work their way through every scrum?"
If you would ask these questions, I would answer, Yes! Ha! Hum!
They pushed, they rushed, they squeezed through in a general sort of way;
But this is where they lost it, Now mark what I shall say,
I found them rush the srimmage, but I did quickly find
The Llanelly men took mighty care the ball was left behind.

'I've seen, but there I know that by this time you are convinced,
That Newport were out manœuvred, although they never flinched,
For after 40 minutes' play we say our hopes were false,
For then the show began, in truth, with a new Llanelly waltz;
But I would mention here as true as England is a nation,
That Newport half-back, Harding, has missed his avocation;
A job has now been found for him, an Usk Newportian vows,
A permanent situation in a cattle slaughter-house.

Then, facing Mr Backer with an angry frown and stare,
Tom was horror-struck to find his hat supported by his hair,
Impossible to move him, turned stupid as a lout,
Murmuring in broken language, 'Take *my* advice, "Shell out."'
His only hope is broken, the cup had gone down west;
The tin-pot gone to the tin-plate town (for years I hope) to rest;
He winked a wunk, he smiled a smole, he laid down on the shore,
And coming cup tie matches will not int'rest him more.

The local newspaper had not long replaced the broadside ballad as the bearer of local news and the tradition of an epic poem in ballad style still greeted major events. This was written to celebrate the winning of the 1866 Welsh Challenge Cup, when Newport were beaten, 45-0.

Three
Maoris and Stars

BEN.DAVIES.   R.T.GABE.   J.STRAND.JONES.   DAN.WALTERS.

The 1890s saw an injection of new blood into the team with players who quickly made their mark on the national side.

The story goes that 'Boomer' Nicholl pulled out of an international against Ireland in 1894 so that his brother, David W. Nicholl, on the back row, fourth from the right, could get his one and only cap with the Welsh forwards. Ireland won the match and the Triple Crown in conditions so bad that the game became known as the 'Ballinafeigh Bog Match.'

GRAND FOOTBALL MATCH!

Batley

(The Crack Yorkshire Cup Team)

v.

Llanelly

On the STRADEY GROUNDS, Llanelly, SATURDAY NEXT, September 19th, 1885. Kick off at 3.30 p m. Admission—SIXPENCE. No Change given at the Gate. Season Tickets may now be had of the Secretary.

Left: Harry Watkins was the Llanelly captain, 1904/5, and was capped for Wales against Scotland in 1904. He was a prominent member of a Llandovery brewing family and enjoyed the high life. Right: An early attempt at an action picture from Stradey Park.

GRAND FOOTBALL MATCHES!
On the STRADEY GROUNDS.

On SATURDAY NEXT, Local Cup Tie—
MORFA RANGERS v. LLANGENNECH.
Kick off at 3 p.m.

ON TUESDAY NEXT—
LLANDILO v. LLANELLY TUESDAY TEAM.
Kick off at 2.30 p.m.

Admission (to each Match) THREEPENCE. No Change given at the gate.

☞ NOTICE.—All Persons found climbing the walls or tresspassing on the adjoining grounds will be prosecuted.

David Harry Bowen dropped a goal which gave Llanelly victory over the Maoris, 3 – 0 in 1888. He rose from pupil to teacher to become headmaster of Bynea school and in his career taught many rugby hopefuls including Rhys Gabe and Jack Auckland.

THE WEEK'S SPORT.

CARDIFF v. LLANELLY.

DEFEAT OF THE " BOLD BLUE AND BLACK."

[By "Forward."]

LOVERING'S ATTEMPT.

The " Scarlets " at last have set the fashion to the world. They have conquered the conquerors. Last Saturday will ever remain a red-letter day in the history of the Llanelly team, for on that day was witnessed a decided turn in the tide of Llanelly's fortunes. Cardiff for the first time during the last three or four years were compelled to eat " humble pie " at the feet of fifteen scarlet jerseyed heroes. Messrs Biggs and Co. arrived in Llanelly with the flush of their notable triumphs over Newport and Cambridge still mantling their countenances, but it was quite another colour when they drove from Stradey a little later in the afternoon.

Left: Percy Lloyd leads a foot rush against Cardiff in 1894. Right: Joe Lovering was a utility forward who never quite made the top grade. In this match, he missed a kick at goal against Cardiff in 1893.

The Box Hat XI – a team of fancy dress cricketers which included a number of early rugby stars: George Watkeys (later the borough surveyor), D.W. Rees (a solicitor), and R.L. Sails (the choirmaster).

C.B. 'Boomer' Nicholl, on the back row, third from the left, was a rugby blue from Cambridge, who shared his rugby between Llanelly and Blackheath and became a member of the Barbarians' committee. He won fifteen caps for Wales between 1891 and 1896. He ended his days as a clergyman in Somerset.

W.J. 'Fishguard' Thomas was one of the hard men of the Llanelly pack. He was the only Welshman who toured Australia, 1887/8, in a team that was the forerunner to the British Lions. He spent most of his working life as a steel sorter in the Burry Extension Works of Richard Thomas and Co. His career lasted long enough for him to play alongside his son, Idwal Thomas.

Jack Evans was one of seven Llanelly players capped by Wales, 1895/6. Later he was courted by the breakaway Northern Union clubs and became a professional in rugby league.

Rhys Gabe in the famous Welsh team which beat the All Blacks in 1905.

D.J. Daniel – 'Dai Sam' to the crowd – was just seventeen when he was part of the team which beat the Maoris, and won eight caps for Wales. He can be seen on the back row, third from the left. One of his five sons, Billy 'Gypsy' Daniel, became a Llanelly folk hero in the boxing ring, knocking out Max Schmeling. The victory was hailed in Llanelly as he achieved this in one round against an opponent who later became the world heavyweight champion.

Cliff Bowen won four caps for Wales before taking a job in Devonport dockyard and moving to Plymouth Albion. He was also a regular member of the Llanelly cricket XI and played county cricket for Carmarthenshire.

Rhys Gabe in Cardiff strip.

John Strand-Jones was one of a series of
clergymen – including a bishop – who
have graced the field for Llanelly. An
Oxford blue, Strand-Jones was the full-
back in the Welsh team which won the
Triple Crown in 1902.

Cliff Bowen, seated on the right, during
the cricket season.

Ben Davies was the half-back partner of the great Owen Badger.

Dan Walters, one of the Seaside Stars' influx who gained national honours, went on to run a pub in later life.

Full-back, John Strand-Jones, one of the many clerics to pull on a Scarlets' jersey, was discovered at theological college in Lampeter.

Rhys Gabe, sometimes spelt Gape, was the best of a sporting family from Llangennech. He became a teacher in Cardiff and toured Australia with the British Lions as an amateur.

This Welsh team includes three Scarlets – Conway Rees, Tom Evans and Jim Watts.

Steelworker Jim Watts played eleven times for Wales between 1907 and 1909 which included games against the Springboks in 1906 and Wallabies in 1908. At 5 ft 8 in and weighing 12 st 4 lb he was one of the lightest of the top forwards of his time but he played like a terrier.

The police have proved to be another fertile recruiting ground for the club and the force was often a useful source of employment for amateurs looking for jobs. This police team is from 1913.

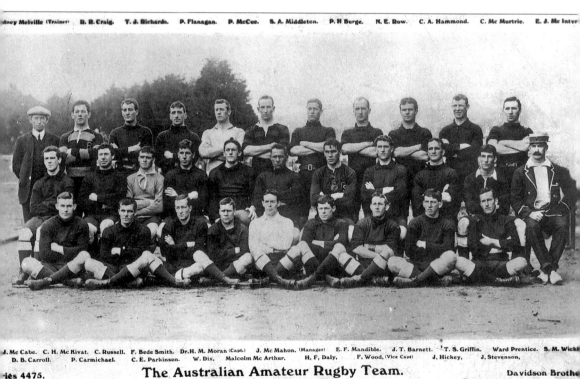

dney Melville (Trainer) R. B. Craig. T. J. Richards. P. Flanagan. P. McCue. S. A. Middleton. P. H. Burge. N. E. Row. C. A. Hammond. C. Mc Murtrie. E. J. Mc Intyr

J. Mc Cabe. C. H. Mc Kivat. C. Russell. F. Bede Smith. Dr. H. M. Moran (Capt.) J. McMahon. (Manager) E. F. Mandible. J. T. Barnett. T. S. Griffin. Ward Prentice. S. M. Wick
D. B. Carroll. P. Carmichael. C. E. Parkinson. W. Dix. Malcolm Mc Arthur, H. F. Daly, F. Wood, (Vice Capt) J. Hickey, J. Stevenson,

ies 4475.   The Australian Amateur Rugby Team.   Davidson Broth
                                    "THE WALLABIES."

The 1908 Wallabies side – the Australians were the first national team to crack under the pressure of the Stradey crowd and the relentless running rugby of Llanelly.

In 1906 Llanelly played the touring South African team before a crowd estimated at 20,000. They lost, 16–3. The team was: Gordon Thomas, Rhys Gabe, Will Arnold, Griff Rowe, Willie Thomas, Harvey Thomas, Dai Lloyd, Dan Walters (captain), Tom Evans, Jim Watts, Harry Watkins, Lt Dobbs, Harry Cole, Will Cole, and Jack Auckland.

Seven Randall brothers made up an entire team in a seven-a-side tournament in Carmarthen in 1907.

The Scarlets have always tried to identify talent at an early age and Llanelly schoolboy sides have usually been strong. This 1907 side includes Bryn Williams, seated second from right, and Edgar Morgan, standing on the extreme right.

A.J. Stacey, ever-present in the pack in the 1900s, went on to become a Welsh bowls international. His name is remembered even now, in a bowls competition still played today.

The legend of Llanelly, the giant killers, was really established in October 1908 when this team beat the Australian XV, 8 – 3. Winger Handel Richards scored a try in the first half and another was scored by forward Tom Evans in the second. The characters are, on the back row, from left to right: T.R. Mills (chairman), Jim Watts, Jack Auckland, D. Llewellyn Bowen, A.J. Stacey, Will Cole, Ike Lewis, W.J. 'Fishguard' Thomas, and Tom Miller (committeeman). On the middle row: Handel Richards, Revd Tom Williams, Tom Evans (captain), Harvey Thomas, and Will Thomas. On the front row: Dai Lloyd, Harry Morgan, Willie Arnold, and W.H. 'Mabon' Davies (trainer).

This is the earliest action shot from Stradey, showing a lineout in the match against the Wallabies in 1908.

Jack Auckland followed a successful playing career in the Scarlets' pack with a spell as an influential administrator in the 1920s.

The Llanelly Oriental Stars R.F.C. and their Opponents at Bordeaux.

The Llanelly Oriental Stars were one of the many minor teams which fed the town with talent.

John Pugh, standing in the suit and tie, was an energetic forward before the First World War and became one of the town's most successful businessmen.

Hubert John, in the middle of the front row, was for many years was captain of Llanelly's cricket XI, but also played as a centre for the rugby side.

Llanelly, 1913/14, the last season before the First World War.

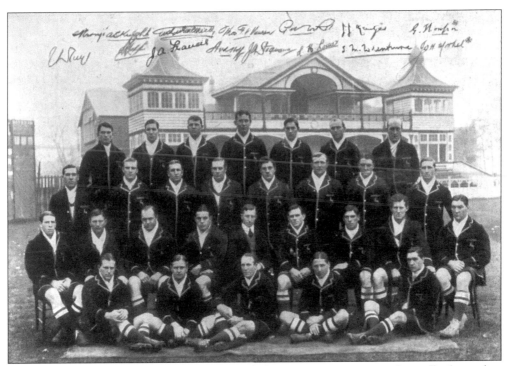

The 1912 Springboks swept all before them before coming up against the wall of sound at Stradey. One of the reporters covering the match wrote: 'The spectators create an atmosphere which is charged with electricity and which, while it unnerves players and spectators who are strangers to Stradey, acts as a powerful stimulus upon the Llanelly players and inspires them to put forward efforts almost superhuman'.

Owen Davies was in the centre when a heroic Llanelly team went down, 7–8, against the 1912 Springboks. How flimsy-looking his jersey seems when compared with modern fabrics.

The First World War has produced many tales of communities and work mates enlisting *en masse*. New Dock Stars heard Lord Kitchener's call and went to the recruiting office together.

Four

All Roads Lead to
Stradey Park

The gates of the ground, as it stands today, date back only to 1972. The local council met the cost as a commemoration of the centenary of rugby in the town.

Stradey Park in the 1930s. The wasteland behind the stand was later turned into a training ground.

The club badge was designed by local artist Vernon Hurford.

This picture was taken soon after the Second World War. The ground can be seen at bottom centre.

Llanelli art school in Coleshill Terrace was originally the Scarlets' gymnasium. It was set up in 1892, after criticism of the Llanelly forwards' fitness. Cardiff and Newport players always seemed in far better condition, it was said.

Stradey in 1964, partly hidden by the smoke of Llanelly Steel.

"No it's not haymaking time".
Just some of the helpers spreading straw at Stradey.

Even the girls help at the Stradey clean-up.

There were hard winters in years gone by. Often rugby would be out the question for several weeks around Christmas with the ground covered in snow and rock hard through frost. Sometimes big efforts had to be made to get the ground ready for an important match. Keeping the ground warm with a covering of straw was one method tried.

Arthur Gould, the great Newport centre, was the hero of the Wales *v.* Ireland international match at Stradey in 1893 – not because of his play, but because he shinned up the posts to replace the crossbar after it had collapsed under the weight of driving snow.

Below: The Scarlets seemed on the way to oblivion in the early 1890s, but were rejuvenated by a merger with the Seaside Stars, a working men's rugby club. Together, they formed a team so strong that, within a year, four of their number had been capped for Wales. It was the first time the club had really embraced ordinary working men. Dai Morgan worked at the St David's Tinplate Works, while Owen Badger, one of the first to be enticed to Rugby League, was a shearer at Burry Works.

Llanelli has always had its own way of doing things, so it will come as no surprise that the Llanelli Wanderers had their own ground, also at Stradey. This is a Wanderers' side from 1962. With them are the members of the international XV, including Ray Williams (back row, fourth from the left), R.H. Williams (seated, third from the left), Carwyn James (front row, centre) and Cliff Morgan (front row, second from the left).

The Llanelli Wanderers' ground was on the opposite side of the cricket field and covered part of the area that was the nineteenth-century rugby field. The original wall of Stradey is seen in the background and the original gates are behind the club house. The Wanderers were originally part of Llanelly YMCA, but broke away in 1950.

The original gates of Stradey Park. Immediately behind them is the current Llanelly Wanderers' ground which covers the area where early matches were played. The cricket ground is away to the left with the present rugby ground in front of it.

Stradey Park today, clustered around with houses, caravans and industrial buildings.

Spectators heading for Stradey would have had a very different walk before 1922. The railway line and the gates can be seen in the background here.

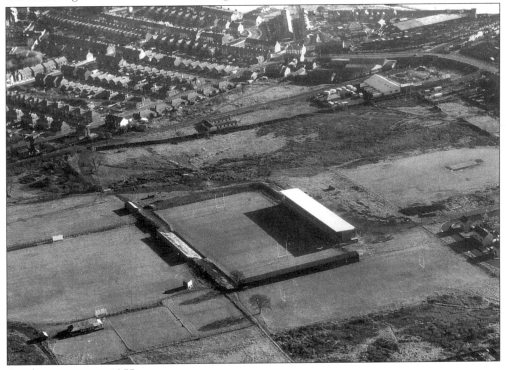

Stradey as it was in 1957.

There is no sign here of Stradey Park Avenue or Chapman Street. The girders are thought to have come from the demolished Stradey Foundry which disappeared some time after 1913.

This much changed view looks across the railway from Stradey Park Avenue to the area now occupied by the club's car park.

Stradey Park was leased from the squire of Stradey, who was C.W. Mansel Lewis, until after the Second World War when the club raised the money to buy it. Mansel Lewis was always a strong supporter of rugby and fought off pressure from developers who wanted to build on the land. However, one requirement of the lease was that the ground should be available for summer shows and it was not always left in a fit state for rugby. In one horse show the water jump was dug on the halfway line and when the Royal Welsh Show, which was attended by the Prince of Wales, came there in 1930 there were complaints afterwards that the rugby ground was badly dug up.

In 1912, the ground provided a suitable landing for Monsieur Salmet, the *Daily Mail* airman, who flew in in his Bleriot monoplane, interrupting a cricket match. Note the rugby stand in the background.

However heavy the tread of the Prince of Wales, he would not have done as much damage as Buffalo Bill and his Wild West Show who visited Stradey in May 1904.

From Llywelyn's last warrior to the King of the Rough Riders. When the Cardiff television company Teliesyn wanted to make a programme about the Wild West Show's visit to Stradey, who better to play Buffalo Bill than that Scarlet hero turned actor, Ray Gravell.

The ground as it is today, with the World Cup stand on the right.

Stradey's Welsh language scoreboard is one of the most intimidating parts of the ground for visitors from across the border. English sides in particular feel stripped of their identity as familiar names like Bath and Gloucester turn into their unfamiliar Welsh counterparts: Caerfaddon and Caerloyw.

Five
Enter Albert Jenkins...

A Llanelly team, 1919/20, pictured at the Town Hall ground. The Revd Alban Davies, the captain, is holding the ball, and Albert Jenkins is the player seated on the far left.

This team, from 1919, rugby after the First World War.

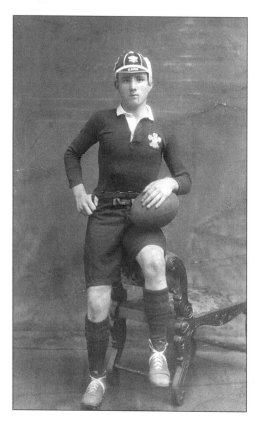

Ronald Protheroe from Stebonheath school was the first to be capped for the Welsh Schools' team.

The four Scarlets selected for the Welsh team, 1919/20 were from left to right: Bryn Evans, Edgar Morgan, Albert Jenkins and Bryn Williams when they played the first matches after the First World War.

Albert Jenkins goes over for a try for Wales against Scotland at Murrayfield in 1928.

Gethin Thomas, later the postmaster at Llwynhendy, was capped for Wales in 1923. He was selected to play in a match held to celebrate the centenary of rugby at Rugby school in the same year, but had to pull out through injury.

The school rugby programme caught them young. Park Street school was right in the centre of the town and did not have any playing fields, but that did not stop them being the champion junior school side, 1921/2.

Sospanville's a vale of desolation,
  Stradey's classic slope is swamped with
    tears,
The "tanner bank's" afire with indig-
  nation,
  Llanelly's off the map; so it appears:
Sospan Fach may flutter brave and bold,
But the Scarlets they are in the cold,'
Not one of them's picked to play for
  Wales.

"Cardiff Arms" may soon spell "consterna-
  tion,"
  Welshmen may exclaim, "We're in the
    muck,
Llanelly might have saved the situation,
  Without them, Wales will never 'break
    her duck'":
Wales, oh! Wales! Llanelly is the town
To bring back home the famous Triple
  Crown,
Or else, we must alter it to "Wails."

'There is a rugby footballer in Llanelly called Albert Jenkins. He is a tinplater by trade, and, in his spare time, since he returned from France a couple of weeks ago after long service, he wins matches for Llanelly by kicking goals and scoring no end of tries. The bigger the match, the better he performs. He is worshipped by the Llanelly crowd, half of whom are attracted week by week simply to see Jenkins display his skill.'
(*South Wales Daily Post*)

Below left: Gwyn Francis played in the first international match after the First World War and later gained a blue at Oxford University. He played at forward for many teams including: Llanelly, London Welsh, and Surrey.
Right: Ike Fowler, an inside-half from Ammanford, played for Wales against the New Zealand Army in 1919. In August that year, however, he signed to play Rugby League for Batley. Wartime shortages had delayed the issue of Welsh caps, and Ike's defection to the professional ranks meant he did not win his cap until 56 years later, when he was eighty-one. He is still living in Yorkshire.

Winger Ernie Finch sent the crowd into paroxysms of delight with a try in the corner against the 1924 All Blacks. Unfortunately, though, he could not stop Llanelly losing an exiting game, 8 – 3. George Nepia the New Zealand full-back became a favourite with the Stradey crowd – perhaps for the two goals he kicked, but more likely because of his despairing, failed attempt to stop Finch.

The Maoris came back to Stradey in November 1926 and were beaten again, 3–0. When the teams went on to the field it seemed that the visitors were not going to perform the haka, but Albert Jenkins ran over to speak to their captain and the traditional war cry rang out to the delight of a 20,000 strong crowd. The only points scored were taken by Sid Hay with an unconverted try. The Llanelly team were: Ewart Thomas, Sid Hay, Tom Evans, Albert Jenkins, Ernie Finch, Cyril Jenkins, Dai John, Ivor Jones (captain), Alf Parker, Fred Harries, Emrys Griffiths, Bobby Evans, F. Rees Thomas, Watcyn Thomas, and Harry Morris.

Can you have too much of Albert Jenkins?
The crowds in the 1920s did not think so
and there was great excitement when it
was rumoured that he would come out of
retirement to meet the 1935 All Blacks.

The top table at the dinner held for the
1927 Waratahs.

Arthur John crosses the line for a try against the Waratahs; Ernie Finch is in support.

Sid Hay receives the ball during the 1926 Maori match as Tom Evans is tackled.

The team that played against the Waratahs. On the back row, from left to right: Alf Parker, Iorwerth Jones, Harry Morris, Jack Williams, Gitto Rees (trainer), Archie Skym, Bryn Evans, Rees Thomas, and Jack Auckland (secretary). Seated: W.J. Davies, Ned Samuel, Oswald Morgan (chairman), Ivor Jones (captain), Frank Rees (president), Albert Jenkins, Ernie Finch, and Ewart Thomas. In front: Arthur John, and Dai John.

The Waratahs on the attack!

Facing page, left: Loughor born Ivor Jones played for Llanelly from 1922 to 1938 and was the star of the British Lions tour of New Zealand in 1930. Right: Idris Jones (centre), was the son of a tinworker, won a blue at Cambridge and went on to captain his club and country. He was the brother of Lord Elwyn Jones who went on to become Lord Chancellor after playing in the prosecuting team at the Nazi war trials at Nuremburg.

The 1927 New South Wales rugby side, known as the Waratahs, beat Llanelly, 24 – 14, in what was described in a local newspaper as 'a dazzling display of football.' Here, Ernie Finch kicks ahead, with Rees Thomas, Alf Parker, Arthur John and Dai John in support.

Seven Scarlets were picked for Wales in 1928. They were, on the back row, from left to right: Arthur John, Ernie Finch, Albert Jenkins, and Dai John. On the front row: Iorwerth Jones, Ivor Jones, and Archie Skym.

Archie Skym, the policeman from Drefach, was capped twenty times for Wales at prop-forward and was a member of the first Welsh team to win a Twickenham.

The Scarlets and the Waratahs scrum down.

Frank Evans, a winger from Dafen, went north after winning his first Welsh cap. He joined Swinton and became a rugby league international and the star of the Great Britain side which toured Australia in 1924.

Six
Little Saucepans

Saucepan making was one Llanelli's biggest industries. Although the workers were mainly women, the pan – 'sosban' in the Welsh, or 'sospan' in Llanelli's home-bred version of 'yr iaith' – quickly became the emblem of the town and its rugby team. Llanelli diehards insist that *Sospan Fach* was written in the bar of the York Hotel, directly opposite the original ground in People's Park. Over the years verses have been added. 'Who beat the Walla-Wallabies' dates back to 1908, while 'Who beat the All Blacks … but good old Sospan Fach,' came in 1972.

The club song's origin has long been claimed by Llanwrtyd Wells, the tiny mid-Wales town. Their Town Council unearthed this early published copy, named 'The Llanwrtyd Anthem' during their centenary celebration in 1995.

"Sospan Bach."

The "Wallabies" were the invaders, and all forces, magic and otherwise, were brought to bear against them, to repel, overcome, and defeat them; and they rejoiced in their hour of triumph. It would have been all so impressive, inspiring and welcome only that for days we had been continually warned to look out for ourselves at Llanelly. They would kick with both feet at the one time, spring upon one like tigers, and maul like a fall of rock in a quarry. But the "Wallabies" were splendidly received by the crowd, and after our warcry had been rendered in defiance they sang their great saucepan song, by which a Llanelly man is known the world over. Fifteen thousand voices sang out with heart and harmony this quaint refrain :—

Mary Ann's sore finger is better,
And David the servant is dead;
The baby in the cradle is quiet,
And the cat is sleeping on her bed.
Sospan bach a boiling on the fire,
Sospan bach a boiling on the fire,
And the cat has scratched Johnny
    very bad.

Above left: In the early days, the team song was reported as *Marching Through Georgia*. However, by 1908 the Llanelly team had established the present nonsense song which is about the misfortunes of a Welsh family while the little saucepan is boiling on the fire. This was the year that the Wallabies arrived in Llanelly and Aussie forward Tom Richards recorded the fans at Stradey singing it in the *Sydney Mail*.
Right: The Llanelly-Llanwrtyd connection is given credence by the fact that the outstanding wing three-quarter in the 1890s, Percy Lloyd, ran a hotel in the spa town.

Deserved to Win.

We fought the famous Llanelly warriors at their own game and on their own "dunghill." They won—deserved to win, too; and the "Children of St. David" celebrated their victory right royally. They shook saucepans and red ribbons at us, shouted and sang 'Saucepan Fach' all along the streets as we drove back to town. Crowds of people densely packed the main thoroughfares at night-time, banging tin cans, taking charge of the tramcars, and singing the everlasting refrain "Sospan Fach." All day long this inspiring tune of witchery was ringing in our ears, and as the train drew out of the station, after dinner with the Llanelly team, everybody was frantically expressing their good wishes and farewells in the same throbbing refrain, "Sospan Fach."

Left: Frank Evans was capped against Scotland in 1921, but was later enticed away to play rugby league with Swinton. Right: Cliff Tanner, seated on the right, was another all-rounder playing behind the scrum in the winter and scoring lots of runs for the cricket club in the summer.

Bryn Evans is among these Welsh forwards practising before a match against England.

Facing page: Jim Lang, the giant Llanelly forward, made his Welsh debut against the 1935 New Zealanders. He is fourth from the left on the back row.

Bryn Evans is coming round to join the ruck while Watcyn Thomas, standing well to the rear, awaits developments. The ball carrier has been tentatively identified as Scarlets' prop, Lewis Elliott.

The Llanelly team, 1934/5.

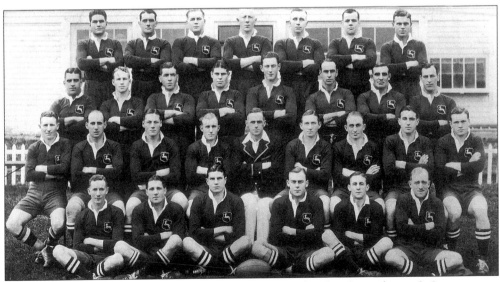

The 1931 South Africans attracted a 19,000 strong crowd to Stradey and won, 9–0.

Elvet Jones (left), the flying winger of the 1930s, was ignored by the Welsh selectors but was one of the stars of the British Lions' tour to South Africa in 1938. There is a street in Llanelli called Heol Elfed, which is named after him. He usually played outside W.H. 'Bill' Clement, who went on to be secretary of the Welsh Rugby Union. Clement (right) was a major in the infantry during the Second World War and was wounded twice. He was heralded as a hero and awarded the Military Cross.

Jim Lang on the charge during a match at Swansea.

Llanelly's side met Northampton in 1935. Prior to the match they were taken on a tour of the Sears and Co. shoe factory in the Midlands town. Peter Dark, Ron Harris, Bill Clement, Stan Jones (secretary), Emrys Davies, Gerald Elias, Elvet Jones, Dai John, and Ivor Jones can be seen admiring the shoes – or more likely, the pretty girls making them.

Bryn Howells comes up to take a pass from Wilf Wooller in a Welsh trial at Swansea.

Watcyn Thomas, the Welsh captain, introduces the Prince of Wales to the rest of his team in 1933.

329. PROPOSED VISIT BY LLANELLI RUGBY FOOTBALL CLUB TO SOUTH AFRICA

The attention of the council was drawn to the contemplated tour of South Africa by the Llanelli Rugby Football Club.

The majority view of the Town Council was that such a tour would be contrary to the traditions of the Club and would cause offence to those who were concerned about the racialist policies in sport.

It was accordingly resolved that the club be requested to have second thoughts on this issue and to decline the invitation in question.

Travelling the world became a more contentious business in the 1970s.

The crowd that saw the 1935 All Blacks beat Llanelly, 16 – 8. Spectators clamoured to watch the match and climbed on to the roof of the cricket pavilion and the refreshment hut. Emrys Davies scored Llanelly's only try.

The 1935 All Blacks perform the haka to an appreciative crowd.

Ivor Jones crosses for a try against New Zealand in 1935.

Bill Clement on the run for Wales.

The visit of the All Blacks was always a great social occasion, as well as a rugby event. Over the years the town has produced All Black bread, cakes in the shape of rugby balls, pop songs and all sorts of souvenirs, both official and unofficial.

The Welsh team takes to the field against Ireland in 1933. Watcyn Thomas, by then a Swansea player, was playing his last international. Edgar Jones, a prop-forward who later went to rugby league, was the only official Llanelly representative although Archie Skym, the policeman forward from Drefach, was also in the side.

Rugby went on through the war years. Several Llanelly players are on view in this wartime international.

The great split between amateur and professional codes was temporarily healed during the Second World War when rugby league players, who had come home to work in the mines and foundries, were allowed to play for their home clubs. This mix of league and union players put on a match at Stebonheath.

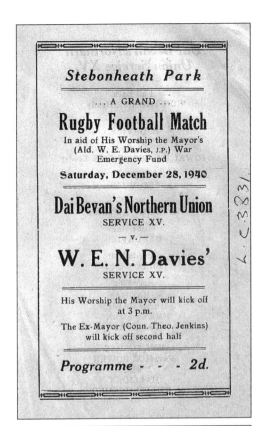

Stebonheath Park

.... A GRAND ....

Rugby Football Match

In aid of His Worship the Mayor's
(Ald. W. E. Davies, J.P.) War
Emergency Fund

Saturday, December 28, 1940

Dai Bevan's Northern Union
SERVICE XV.

— v. —

W. E. N. Davies'
SERVICE XV.

His Worship the Mayor will kick off
at 3 p.m.

The Ex-Mayor (Coun. Theo. Jenkins)
will kick off second half

Programme - - - 2d.

L. C.383/

Dai Bevan's Northern Union Service XV.	W. E. N. Davies' Service XV.
Full Back	Full Back
RON THOMAS, Hendy	CLARKE (R.A.F.)
Wing	Wing
E. DAVIES	HARRIES (Plymouth & R.A.F.)
Centre	Centre
IDWAL DAVIES (Wales & Leeds)	BISHOP (Pontypool & R.A.F.)
Centre	Centre
TED WARD	GWILI JENKINS
Wing	Wing
W. FRANCIS, Furnace	ELVET JONES
Inside Half	Inside Half
DAI DAVIES	RAVALDE (Yorkshire & R.A.F.)
Outside Half	Outside Half
BILLO REES	MORRIS (R.A.F.)
Forwards	Forwards
E. BADHAM	HERBERT (R.A.F.)
BRYN DAVIES	BRYN EVANS
EMRYS EVANS	WATKINS (R.A.F.)
DAI EVANS	RYAN (R.A.F.)
J. RICHARDS	W. J. JONES
W. J. DAVIES	F. L. MORGAN
Rev. H. C. BOWEN	J. L. MORGAN
J. REES	HOWARD DAVIES
HALLIDAY	D. WESTCOTT
EMLYN HUGHES	C. WESTCOTT

England was the opponent in this match from 1943.

The New Zealand All Blacks were the first post-war tourists, beating Llanelly, 16 – 8, in October 1945. Five of the home team were still in the forces. The crowd responded to the New Zealanders' haka with what was described in the local press as ' a full-throated rendering' of *Sospan Fach*.

Seven

Lions and Dragons

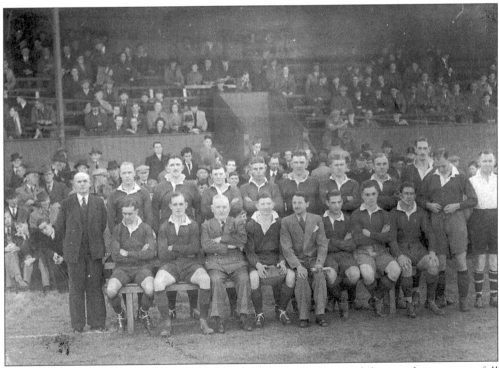

By 1948 many of the players had trickled back from the services and the squad was near to full strength.

Cross Keys at Stradey in 1957. The lineout includes: Henry Morgan (capped), Euros Bowen, John Miles, and R.H. Williams. Wyn Evans and Geoff Howells, the Bynea steelworker who played forty-three times for Wales, look on.

Llanelly, in their reserve strip, meet London Welsh in 1957. Wyn Evans is the scrum-half and R.H. Williams can be seen signalling the move. Aubrey Gale and Glyndwr Jenkins are among players in the lineout.

Peter Davies, a full-back, was Llanelly's top scorer with 122 points. He was the son of the long-time Glamorgan cricketer and Test Match Umpire Emrys Davies. Peter Davies, seen here (left) with the author, went on to a successful career as a London barrister.

Willie Jones, the Glamorgan all-rounder, spent his winters playing at fly-half, first for Llanelly and later for Gloucester.

Two of Stradey's legends are standing with Handel Rogers, the administrator who did most to push the club to world-wide fame. Onllwyn Brace (left), who won an Oxford blue, joined Llanelly in 1957 after taking on a job at the Trostre tinworks. He captained the club from 1959 to 1961. As BBC Head of Sport, he also did much to establish rugby as a television attraction. Rhys Haydn Williams (right), known as R.H., came from Cwmllynfell and captained Llanelly, 1957/8. He played twenty-three times for Wales and was one of the heroes of the British Lions in South Africa, Australia, and New Zealand. His son, Steve, has contributed many of the pictures included in this volume from this era. Postmaster Handel Rogers was behind the Scarlets' trip to Moscow and the other trips abroad which followed. He argued that the club needed to keep a high profile if it was to remain a byword for rugby excellence.

Here is Ossie Williams with the ball and Ken Jones, later the club's long-serving secretary, with his back to the camera, *c.* 1951.

Graham Jefferies, Rhys Williams (Llanelli skipper), Ossie Williams (Springbok lock), Chris Koch, H. Prosser-Jones and two other South Africans can be seen at the party.

The 1951 South African tourists had a successful visit to Stradey, beating the Scarlets,' 20–11. Rhys Williams is seen here having a good time at the after-match party with South African, Ernie Dimpelman.

Stan Williams and Ossie Williams
are among the forwards bearing down
on the trapped Scotsman in this
international.

Selwyn-Williams was a top class
scrum-half for Llanelli's great cup-
winning sides of the 1970s.

Eight

From Stradey to Moscow (and Beyond)

Under the guidance of committeeman Handel Rogers, the club began to travel the world. In 1957, Llanelly became the first British rugby team to play in the Soviet Union. The team was captained by R.H. Williams and included John Brock, Euros Bowen, Cyril Davies, Howard Davies, Peter Davies, Terry Davies, Wynne Evans, Aubrey Gale, Geoff Howells, Carwyn James, Glyndwr Jenkins, Henry Morgan, John Miles, Mike Phillips, Geraint Stephens, Bryan Thomas and Raymond Williams. Here they wait for their train on Llanelly station.

A drinks break at half time. Czechoslovakia were Llanelly's first opponents, and were beaten, 35–9.

The teams line up for the pre-match anthems.

R.H. Williams, standing at the back left with his hands on his hips, casts an eye over a rather imposing trophy.

Cossacks and souvenir sellers.

The Welsh language scoreboard at Stradey Park was thought to be the ultimate in one-up-manship. As this scoreboard shows, this was not so!

A diplomatic incident. The referee can be seen attending to a Rumanian player who has had his ear bitten by a Llanelly forward.

The Scarlets met Rumania twice, drawing, 6–6 the first time, and losing, 6–3 on the second occasion.

Ray Williams was rather surprised to be greeted with flowers.

Home at last! The Mayor greets Ray Williams and Handel Rogers.

Aubrey Gale held up an attempted attack by the University of Toronto in Spring 1965.

Llanelly scrum-half Peter Williams takes the ball from the lineout in Toronto.

Both Terry Davies and his brother Len were capped for Wales. Len died young, but Terry went on to a successful career as a businessman.

Kel Coslett went north to play in a professional side in Rugby League. His younger brother Keri was a stalwart of the side in the late 1970s.

Nine
Kings, Princes and Carwyn

Phil Bennett, the prince of the fly-halves, meeting Duncan Goodhew.

The Llanelli school's team produced top names in Llanelli rugby. Stuart Gallacher, appointed as chief executive when the club became a limited company in the 1990s, is seen here at the start of a career which saw him skipper Llanelli.

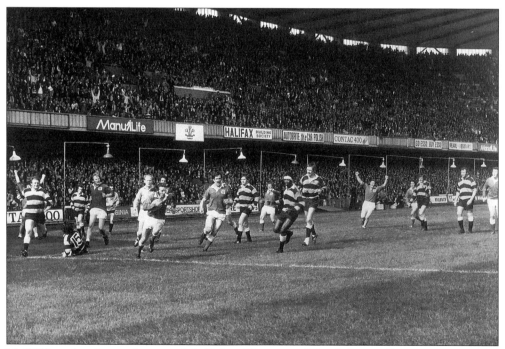

J.J. Williams heads over for a try while Delme Thomas and Derek Quinnell come up in support.

Delme Thomas leaps for the ball.

John Warlow, holding the ball in the middle of this Stebonheath school group, was capped for Wales in the 1960s.

Ben Davies was a Welsh international in the 1890s and later became a coach and committeeman. He was followed into rugby by his sons and thus the family was to be inextricably linked with the club's history. Wilf Davies, known as Major Davies, having achieved distinguished wartime service, was the original 'Scarlet' to write in the Swansea-based *South Wales Evening Post*, and covered major matches at Stradey from the 1920s through to the 1970s.

In the early years, Major Davies' little brother, Harry Davies, would run the copy to the telephone. Later, Harry took over the byline 'Scarlet' himself and was the voice of Llanelli rugby to the outside world through the 1980s and beyond. He also followed in his father's footsteps as a distinguished scrum-half, playing for Felinfoel and came close to selection against the 1935 All Blacks.

Carwyn James, on the back row, fourth from the left, was an unusual rugby player. He was a cultured, poetical man who proved, as Llanelli and British Lions coach, that an incisive brain could triumph over any amount of muscle. In 1970 he turned his attention to the political scene and stood for parliament as a Plaid Cymru candidate.

Carwyn, sitting on the left, was one of those superb players whose path to national honours was blocked by a rival, (Cliff Morgan), who reached the peak of rugby genius. No-one, though, saw more of what was going on inside the game.

Delme Thomas, Tommy David, and Gareth Jenkins in a lineout at Cardiff Arms Park.

Ray Gravell and Derek Quinnell helped out in a charity cricket match.

A Cup Final try at Cardiff Arms Park.

Alistair Hignell, the England full-back, is tackled at Stradey in the 1970s.

The King – Barry John. Barry John soon moved from Llanelli to Cardiff to follow his career but left behind two talented brothers and a sister who was to marry Derek Quinnell, thereby founding a rugby dynasty.

In the dry, those feet would twinkle and the opposition forwards would be left clutching at thin air.

MOSELEY

v.

LLANELLI

MOSELEY
(Red & Black)   **LLANELLI**

MOSELEY				LLANELLI
S. A. DOBLE	15	*Full Back*	C. GRIFFITHS	15
R. WAIN	14	*Right Wing*	C. HERBERT	14
A. W. HILL	13	*Right Centre*	F. FENDER	13
C. W. McFADYEAN	12	*Left Centre*	W. WILLIAMS	12
A. THOMAS	11	*Left Wing*	T. DAVIES	11
J. F. FINLAN	10	*Fly Half*	B. THOMAS	10
P. J. KINGSTON	9	*Scrum Half*	S. WILLIAMS	9
J. H. DAWSON	1	*Forwards*	T. CROCKER	1
D. PROTHEROUGH	2	,,	H. THOMAS	2
B. GREAVES	3	,,	B. LLEWELYN	3
B. AYRE	4	,,	W. D. THOMAS	4
D. MASON	5	,,	R. POWELL	5
M. J. GREEN	6	,,	G. THOMAS	6
J. C. WHITE	8	,,	G. JENKINS	8
D. WARREN	7	,,	M. GRIFFITHS	7

Referee: R. A. ELLIS (Gloucester)

The ball for this afternoons match has very kindly been presented by BURNSALL METAL FINISHERS LTD. 67, Northwood Street, Birmingham, B3 1TX.

Sat.   12th January at the Reddings: 1st XV v. N'HAMPTON   2.30 p.m
Sat.   19th January   ,,   ,,   1st XV v. SALE   2.30 p.m

Owing to the National Emergency it has not been possible to produce our usual full scale programme.

National emergency – the three day week and power cuts.

The 1963 All Blacks were well fed, but still beat Llanelli, 25 – 8.

Reception Dinner
for the 1963-64 New Zealand Rugby Tourists
at the Stepney Hotel, Llanelly
on Tuesday 31st December 1963

Roy 'Shanto' Thomas, from Penclawdd, never gained representative honours, but is still a legendary figure.

The 1972/3 squad.

Gareth Jenkins, on the back row third from the left, was a member of the team that beat the All Blacks and went on to become a coach.